THE BOOK OF LOVE

THE BOOK OF LOVE

A GUIDE TO THE ESSENCE OF LOVE

KEN BANKS

Copyright © 2003 by Ken Banks
ISBN: 1-4134-3828-8

All rights reserved. No part of this book may be reproduced or transmitted in any form or by any means, electronic or mechanical, including photocopying, recording, or by any information storage and retrieval system, without permission in writing from the author.

This book was printed in the United States of America.

INTRODUCTION

This portion of the book is the most difficult for me to write. It means that if I am going to be honest with you the reader and to myself I have to be truthful. Yet to be truthful is to invite criticism and ridicule from those who would doubt the source of these sayings.

I will tell you now that the only words I can truly claim to be my own are this introduction and the book summary. Everything else within, including the title, came in the form of inspired writings from a spiritual source that I will call God.

The process began in June of 2001. I had just returned home from a great night out with my wife Gloria, when shortly after retiring, I was almost catapulted out of bed with an inner voice that required me to grab pen and paper and begin to write. The words that were written were not my own, but rather words that seemed to flow into my mind. I was merely recording the words as they were given to me.

For many months these "transmissions" came almost daily and I quickly recorded many hundreds of handwritten pages. Although most of the time the words flowed to me without prompting, there were occasions when I asked, and had answered, specific questions. Other than those few passages that begin with a question, all other words are from God and are written from that perspective. So, when the pronoun I is used, God is referring to him/herself.

There will be many doubters as to the authenticity of these sayings. And to that I can offer no proof. You will look to my personal life to determine if I deserve such a blessing, and I can assure you that given my multitude of frailties, you would answer that I do not. I can only say that should you find solace in these words, what difference does it make from whence they came? If these words lead you to a greater understanding of love and how it relates to you, then it would have served its intended purpose.

The Book of Love is the first of four books that I have been given to publish. The others are the Book of Knowledge, The Book of Creation and the Book of Life. It is my hope that the knowledge contained within these books will be a catalyst for the world to begin to understand that we are in fact spiritual beings masquerading as physical beings.

If we could release the ego, and begin to behave like the eternal spiritual beings that we truly are, then perhaps we would begin to treat others as we would like to be treated. Perhaps we would make political and economic decisions based on it being in the best interest of mankind rather then the best interest of an individual or a corporation.

Ultimately, the ability to change the world and ourselves lies with us, as God says many times within the various books "The choice is yours".

*prepare thy mind for love
make fertile the ground upon which
to plant the seeds of love
make way for the fields of love
harvest the crop of love
pollinate your world with the spirit of love*

love is all there is

What is love?

*Love is life's essence
it is the source
without love there is naught*

What can be done without love?

*I tell you that birds do not fly without love
Fish do not swim
Clouds do not form
Seasons do not come and go
Planets do not revolve
Suns do not shine
The universe does not exist
I am that which is love*

Behold

love is the answer to all prayers
love is cherished in heaven and earth
love is relished by the sick
love is desired by children
love is admired
love is inspiring
love is nurturing
love is the essence of all that is
love truly does make the world go round
love is the epitome of thought
love is the light of ages
love is the reason for living
love expresses
love caresses
love becomes
love swallows hate
love dispels fear
love is the absence of fear
love provides
love is to allow others to be
who they are
love is to shower others in light
love is to shine through cloudy skies
love is the beginning of the circle
love is eternity
love endureth
love becomes love

love is the beginning of all things

love was before the beginning
of things
love encompasses all
love envelops all that is and all
that is not
love surrounds all that was and
all that has yet to be
I thought love and you became

what is love?

love is divine ecstasy
love is joy in your heart
love is fulfillment
love is the energy of life

A woman boldly walked up to the master and said, "Tell me what love is. Sometimes I think that I am in love, but then I find that I am not. How can I stay in love?" The master replied, "Imagine that love did not come in from without but flowed out from within. Imagine that your every thought is of love. Imagine that you ecstatically give love to everything and everyone that you ever come in contact with. How then could you lose love?"

*I can speak of love
but ultimately love is a feeling
you are love
go within
feel the love which surges in you
which resonates at the core of you
go deep
who are you?
when you discover/know the answer
you will find love*

where do I find love?

love is in you
love is throughout things
you cannot love one and not the other
it is impossible
we are all one

there is no separation
therefore
just love
it is a state of being
love is not attached to a
particular thing

what of those who love me?

*they will still love or they won't
I tell you this
love that binds is a false love
a possessive love*

*love that allows is as God's love
for you*

love yourself

it is curious that
Upon the earth,
love of yourself is considered
vain or unseemly.
You will say things like
"She is so in love with
herself."
But I say to you
Love yourself grandly
and
forgive yourself
and
release all guilt and shame
these are emotions that
you have created based upon
your understanding of the world
they are not found
in ultimate reality
God is joy, bliss, peace
and love

notice that I did not say
God feels joy, bliss,
peace and love.
Feelings are interpretations
of events.
I am joy
I am bliss
I am peace
I am love
I am these things —
there is not a need to interpret

therefore:
these things are you also
for you and I are one
When Jesus said
"I and the father are one"
he was not speaking individually
but collectively

you are one with God
and since one of
God's qualities is love
when you are love

*you are therefore close
to your true divine nature.*

*when you understand that
we are all one
you will see that love of yourself
means love
of all creation
and the consciousness
supporting creation.*

*then will your love
not be directed toward
a particular thing
as in love of this or
love of that
but rather love
of all that is*

*when this occurs
(and it will occur)
in your consciousness,
then will you be love.
love and consciousness
will be the same
and you will be
one with your divine being.*

all is love
all is one
follow me
I will show you love
love you cannot imagine
follow your heart

*love is
grander than
what you have imagined
it to be*

love is the beginning
prior to the physical universe, love existed
love sustained love
love is the same today
nothing else is needed for love to exist
love has no requirements
no special conditions
love need not be returned
it is its own source
love expands out from within
it cannot be stopped
cannot be contained

*love is the sum of all
things
all experiences
all emotions
all knowledge
all*

speak the word of love
send out waves of love
bury your heart in love
listen to the sound of love
know the heat of love

love when the music is not sweet
love when the tide is not in

lovingness is an art
we are made of love
born in love
free in love
beingness is love
love is art

what is love?
love is the expansion of
the soul
love sustains life
love binds the infinite
love creates
love, God, life, you
it is all the same
we are love

love is what you wish to be surrounded by
to love is to protect
to hold
to cherish
to respect
to honor

to seek to be near

compare love vs. fear
which brings fear?
which brings joy?
which brings peace?
which engages the heart, the spirit?
which dances in the moonlight?
which sings the song?
inspires the artist?
teaches the children?

encourages
picks the best and highest
fathers the cause
mothers the child
relinquishes guilt fear envy doubt anxiety tension
which manages the smile
which brings the peace
which endures the pain

which is aware of all
which feels good
which enlightens
which establishes me
which becomes
which buries hate
which understands
which becomes one

relax

*let go of fears
thou cannot be harmed unless thou chooses
thou art God*

The master and some of his followers were in a small boat at sea, when a violent storm suddenly appeared. The boat looked to be in danger of capsizing. Men and women were screaming; fearing for their lives. Yet the master was calm. A man then grabbed the master by the sleeve and wailed, "Master, are we going to die?" The master stood up, looked upon the water and said, "Be calm." Immediately the winds stopped, the seas became calm and the sun reappeared.

Then the master said, "Have I not said the outer condition reflects perfectly your inner condition. The storm that you see is within your heart. The fear that you feel is within your mind. Therefore, change your heart to be at peace. Change your mind to think of love."

*there is great
catastrophic danger if
your thoughts, beliefs and acts
remain rooted in fear.
There will be great
joy upon the earth
if your thoughts, words and deeds
are rooted in love*

*as always the choice is yours.
you are in a constant state of choice.
Choose always
love over fear.*

*there are worlds
in the universe
where there is
no contention
no strife
no anger
no mistrust
no hatred*

*these beings
prefer
agreement over
contention
calmness over strife
joy over anger
trust for mistrust
love over all*

I tell you that:
the kingdom of heaven is within
your being resides in heaven
you not only reside in heaven
you are heaven
you need only to realize
(to see with real eyes)
who you are in spirit.

the path to realization lies
in love

*God and much of creation
exists in joy, love and bliss.
you can join us whenever you wish*

*Know that you are loved by the All
in a way that is far beyond
human understanding
nothing, nothing you have ever done
or will ever do could cause the
slightest ripple in our love for you
you and all of humanity is treasured
in my eyes. Sacred perfection
manifesting perfection
a complete, whole and harmonious
part of creation*

Father please speak:

*behold the beauty of manifestation
you may choose to behold beauty
or choose to behold ugliness or chaos
or whatever you wish
the beholding is done by you
you get to choose your perceptions
but if it is beauty and love that
you seek, it is but a thought away*

*try being love
be love, before defining
what to love
be love, before attaching
to a person, place or thing*

emanate love
radiate love
explode in love
pulsate love
rain love on others
allow love to reign
when in doubt, love
love when you are content
love when discontent
lovingness is godliness
seek God and find love

practice love.

make thy first thought love
love in every instant
every situation
never recoil from the chance to love
never fail the chance to love
seek love
understand love
open up
stop holding back
allow yourself to be
relax

*love can cure illness
sustain the battle
encourage the masses
build bridges
see beyond the effect
defeat fear
conquer doubt
relay feelings
accomplish great feats
heal the wound
see God*

*see me in everything
in the great and small
praise all of it
bless it
adore it
I am the light within*

who are you?

*the knowing of that will bring you to me
have fun
enjoy everything
love everything*

the word is love
the thought is love
the feeling is love
be thou love
love is the desire of the heart
love conquers hate
love is all that is

fill your being with love
love is not a concept, it is a tangible
feel love
taste love
be love

*the more it is experienced
the more it is sought*

love always

love thy body
it is love expressed
love all that is
it is God

love thy enemy
for there is no enemy save that which you create

*seek love, my son.
you and I are creating together
allow yourself to think grandly
anything is possible!*

*choose according to thy desires
sing the song of the heart
hear the music of the wind
produce ye all things you so desire
for you and I are one
and the same.*

*observe in love
and wonder
at who you are*

*the detached observer sees
but does not judge
do not allow what you perceive
to take you away
from the state of love*

*your nature,
your very being
the truest essence of you,
is woven in love
was created in love
exists in love*

*your task, is to seek love at all times
in all things, in all ways.
be who you are. be love*

to know thyself,
find love

love is the answer

it is the answer
in every instant
every situation
every moment in time
every mention of thought
every battle
every friendship
every collaboration

release into love

the circle is complete

love begins the circle
love ends the circle
love is the circle

*as it is the nature of fish to swim
and the nature of birds to fly,
so it is your nature to love*

*pure love
is the love of all —*

*everything
including yourself*

why do you fret so?
believe that nothing can harm you
and nothing will
I am the life giver
the sustainer
Yet, I sustain according to
your will
for it is your will that I follow
In fact the entire universe
follows your idea of yourself
listen!
thy will be done
on Earth as it is in heaven

*that does not mean
my (God's) will being done
but your will being done
so do not fret
create
express who you love to be
not who you fear to be
love is the answer
find love as a state of being
live love*

you are completely loved

*at all times, in all ways
you are treasured
in my eyes*

*I love every fiber of
your being
every beat of your heart
every breath
every thought
every creation*

*who you are is who I love
no conditions
no requirements*

I tell you this:

Do as I do
Love all things
Love everything and everybody
Love all that you can perceive
Love everything that comes into
your experience
give love at all times

love the all — which is to say
love yourself
love every manifestation of
yourself

when the world is
viewed thus
will the son of God
walk upon the earth

love transcends

how can peace on earth be achieved?

By loving one another

www.ingramcontent.com/pod-product-compliance
Lightning Source LLC
Chambersburg PA
CBHW032136090426
42743CB00007B/614